THE WISE MEN FOLLOW THE STAR TO BETHLEHEM

LILLIE MAE HIPPS-DICKERSON

BALBOA
PRESS

A DIVISION OF HAY HOUSE

Balboa Press books may be ordered through booksellers or by contacting:

Balboa Press
A Division of Hay House
1663 Liberty Drive
Bloomington, IN 47403
www.balboapress.com
1 (877) 407-4847

Because of the dynamic nature of the Internet, any web addresses or links contained in this book may have changed since publication and may no longer be valid. The views expressed in this work are solely those of the author and do not necessarily reflect the views of the publisher, and the publisher hereby disclaims any responsibility for them.

The author of this book does not dispense medical advice or prescribe the use of any technique as a form of treatment for physical, emotional, or medical problems without the advice of a physician, either directly or indirectly. The intent of the author is only to offer information of a general nature to help you in your quest for emotional and spiritual well-being. In the event you use any of the information in this book for yourself, which is your constitutional right, the author and the publisher assume no responsibility for your actions.

Any people depicted in stock imagery provided by Getty Images are models, and such images are being used for illustrative purposes only.
Certain stock imagery © Getty Images.

Print information available on the last page.

ISBN: 978-1-9822-2782-1 (sc)
ISBN: 978-1-9822-2781-4 (e)

Balboa Press rev. date: 05/03/2019

Dedicated to my son, Brian Keith Hipps

Table of Contents

1

MY LIFE ARE UPON A HILL

The elder heard a tiny recording in
Heaven playing a hymn in glory
My life went out over the land in
Wisdom
My life is upon a hill
A small beam of light shine all
Round the Christmas tree in
Holiness City for the new baby
To be praise by the wise men o

Heaven
My life is upon a hill
I worship in the Christmas spirit for
The new baby to be a Savior to all the
Congregation in the world to be a
Christmas gift for everyone in love
My life is upon a hill

2

A CHRISTMAS DREAM

Jesus spoken to me in the precious
Spirit of a dream for me to become
    Free in a Christmas blessing for
        My salvation
      A Christmas Dream
Jesus unwrapping my heart in a
Christmas dream for the world to
  See my pain of happiness
  A Christmas dreams
He placed a Christmas dream in mind
Heart for me to be hold again with
His love that dwell in my life
A Christmas dreams
    A Christmas dreams that full
        My soul with the holy spirit
            Of holiness

3

A SALVATION CHRISTMAS

In the marvelous spirit of the
Spoken word came an angel to
Call all the holy shepherd to come
See a Savior of Christmas
God anoint you to become the
Savior of Christmas for the world
To see the shining light of his salvation
    A Savior Christmas
He shall not reject your soul
From the holiness of salvation
  That someday you will be a
  Christmas gift to someone in
    His precious wisdom of holiness
      In a Savior Christmas

4

IN THE SPIRIT OF CHRISTMAS

I embrace the power in peace for the
Spirit of a Christmas miracle to connected
All the wisdom to the new baby that
Came into the everlasting door of
Heaven with grace
In the spirit of Christmas
I believe in the spirit of Christmas
With a blessing that fall from the
Lord holy hand in a powerful
    Spirit
In the spirit of Christmas
God wrapping his precious love
Around the world for a little
  Blessing for a Christmas in
      Your heart
In the spirit of Christmas

5

SWADDLING CHRISTMAS

There came a shepherd to tell the
　　People a Savior have come to save
　　　　The congregation of the world
　　　　　　Swaddling Christmas
A feast was for the whole congregation
In the holy place to be at peace on
　　　　　A swaddling Christmas
A few of the Lord disciples came out to
　　Meet with the children on the battle
　　　　Field for a swaddling Christmas

6

A SHINE CHRISTMAS TREE

I justified the shine Christmas tree in
 The temple of hope when the Holy Ghost
  Stand under heaven with a silver star
   That bright up in the church of
       Peace
  A shine Christmas tree
A little miracle pours down from heaven
 With a snow flake in designed into a
  Prayer in your heart on Christmas
   A shine Christmas tree
I justified the precious power that shine
  Down on the Christmas tree in
   The church of heaven
    A shine Christmas

7

A CHRISTMAS DROP

A saint went out into the wilderness
To watch over the shepherd in the field
Of peace for a gift to the congregation
Christmas drop
God drop down a tiny Christmas wish for
You to be judge by the angels in the
Center of your soul with a blessing of
A holy gift in the Christmas rain drop
Full of faith that came in the midst
Of your Christmas miracle that fall
Down from heaven
Christmas drops, Christmas blessing

8

I STAND ON A MOUNTAIN

God place two golden tables in my hand for
An offering on Christmas
I stand on a mountain
I dance around the Christmas mistletoe
With all the peaceful angels in the
Wilderness of the temple
I rose up in the spirit of a gift for a
Little Christmas wish that came into
My life with tiny piece of golden salvation
On Christmas morning
I stand on a mountain
I stand on a mountain of Christmas with
the precious shepherd in the Holy Town
Of Bethlehem

9

BRING ME A GIFT

Forsake the power in my gift of a
    Silver Christmas faith
        Bring me a gift
The Lord bring down a gift on Christmas
For me to be joyful in his faith
        Bring me a gift
As the Lord bring me a gift of a precious
Christmas blessing for me to hold in mind
Heart Bring me a gift

10

HAPPINESS MEAN SO MUCH TYO ME

I humbled a rock in a crack of Christmas
  Forsaking the commandment of the spirits
    Of worship to you in the temple
  Happiness mean so much so to me
Your life can be short in the Christmas power
  Of prayer when it come to the edge of a
  Moment in wisdom as you discovered the
  Large Christmas tree in the wilderness of
    Worship when you praise the new baby
    Laid under the bright star for a Christmas
      Miracle for the congregation in the temple

11

THE KING CHRISTMAS HOUSE

All manner of prayer came into the
Holy City of peace for a Christmas
  Miracle that burnt in the middle of
  A bush in a small faith in my gift on
        Christmas morning
        The king Christmas house
The king brought in a gift for the
Little children from house of Christmas
        The king Christmas house
The king call for the shepherd to giving
The gift to all the children of Bethlehem

12

SNOWING THE HOLY SPIRIT

Come again into the holy spirit of
Christmas holiness to see the snow
     Fall from heaven
The holy saint allowed you to be
Praise by the precious power in the
Power in the hand of Jesus because
He returned to see the big Christmas
Tree in the holy spirit of happiness
     It is snow in the temple of grace
       That came upon the town of
      Bethlehem so you can be blessing
       By the holy spirit of Christmas

13

CONSUMED YOUR GIFT

Stretch forth the Christmas sea as you
    Cry for peace to come into your heart
        Consumed your gift
God walked around the blue Christmas
  Flag that went up the pole for the world
      To see him love
        Consumed your gift
God wash me in his Christmas snow with
    His precious spirit of power as a gift
      Before his congregation of happiness
      Consumed your gift
The sight of a Christmas salvation shall come
  Into your life with a scale full of faith that
      Fill your heart
      Consumed your gift

14

A WORD IN THE CHRISTMAS PRAYER

In your preacher word are a prison that are
March into the freedom of Christmas prayer
      From heaven
  A word in Christmas prayer
I will pass across the heaven river in
The temple of peace that went out into
Someone life with a Christmas offer
    Before the Lord
    A word in Christmas prayer
I believed in the journey of a silver
Moment on Christmas day as I minister
To the saints in the vineyard Of grace

15

CAST OUT A CHRISTMAS WISH

A holy angel went straight up to the open
      Door of Christmas in heaven
   Cast out a Christmas wish
The gospel field of Christmas was full of
Christmas presents for the little children
In the vineyard of wisdom for them to see
The new baby in Bethlehem
Cast out a Christmas wish
My wish came together for a word from
    The Lord on Christmas
I cast out a tiny blessing in a Christmas prayer
To the Lord

16

SAT DOWN

6he elder went and sat down at the
Foot of the cross and cry and his tears
On a Christmas star for a moment in the
      Holy salvation of peace
The blissful name is in a wish on Christmas
Day with the angels that came into the someone
Heart with peace to pray for a moment of love
That came upon a shine star on Christmas as
      I sat down at the foot of the cross

17

DEPARTED IN A BLESSING

A Christmas reflection on a blessing
 In my heart with the Lord glory
  Departed in a blessing
As I walk in the wilderness of his grace and
The Christmas angels came into the holy city
With a vessel of faith in their hands for the
Blessing to the temple for Christmas miracle
  Departed in a blessing
All holy angels laid out their Christmas
Gift to the saints in the wilderness
  Departed in a blessing of Christmas miracle
For the new baby in Bethlehem

18

IN THE CHRISTMAS

In the highest of the season a small voice
Fall from the kingdom in prayer for you
    In the Christmas miracle
       In the Christmas glory
The shepherd minister to the
Congregation to receiver the Lord
Gift for someone that have a course
On the Christmas road of grace to you
    In the Christmas gospel
       In the Christmas of thankful

19

PEACE TO CHRISTMAS

Your peace come to you in the
Christmas miracle when everything
Go out into the world with the gospel
In praise of a Christmas blessing
       Peace to Christmas
Keep yourself clean in the eyes of
A Christmas peace with the holy
   Angels in heaven
     Peace to Christmas
Your peace come to you in a Christmas
Miracle for you to be blessing in the spirit
Of wisdom Peace to Christmas

20

DISCILE CHRISTMAS

Personal your religion in a traveling power
Of golden picture with all the faith in a
Disciple Christmas
Disciple Christmas
A disciple Christmas came a long way
With a gift in holiness of freedom for you
To be happy for a Christmas blessing
Disciple Christmas
I worship in the grace of Christmas
When I rose up for a piece of my heart
To go up into heaven in the spirit for a
Christmas blessing
Disciple Christmas

21

EARTH QUAKED IN CHRISTMAS

My name is upon altar of prayer
As I journey with the host of the temple
    In the air of my salvation
    Earth quaked in Christmas
A prophet sent out a word of power
  For you to praise the Christmas spirit
    With all the preacher on the road
      To the earth quaked in the earth quake
        In your Christmas gift for the little
         Children of Bethlehem
        Earth quake Christmas

22

DELIVERED CHRISTMAS

Amen are in the spirit of delivered
Christmas when you end your prayer
Of thank to the holy worshipping as you
    Lift your voice to the Lord for your
        Christmas gift to the congregation
           In the church
           Delivered Christmas
    Your delivered to the church is in the
Christmas dance for the praise in your soul

23

LET US KNEE DOWN

Confound the gospel book in the
 Christmas presence of the glory
  Let us knee down
My Christmas are not a stumbling
Block at the base of a in my soul,
A matter of the right word done
In the creature of a Christmas cross
  Let us knee down
My reward is a kneel of faith in
The sack clothes of a shine stone
  On Christmas
Hollowed be in my Christmas daily
Praise for the holy one in 6the spirit
  Let us knee down

24

WATER DOWN CHRISTMAS

When I water down my Christmas to
Recover my life in the Lord salvation
I shall receiver my reward in the
Silver prayer
Water down Christmas
A small voice came up out of the
Water a living spirit for your Christmas
Present and for you to be a witness of the
Holy Ghost in the land of wisdom that hold
You together in the Lord love
Water down Christmas

25

A POWERFUL WITNESS

The uttermost praise is a big part
Of your faith in a Christmas grace for
Your testimony due to the open spirit
In your wisdom for a gift that came into
        Your heart
    A powerful witness
Sometimes I wrestle with my life
Because some of us feel like a year
A part for our family but I hope that
One day we will come together in the
Lord love for a Christmas story to be
  Told in their life A powerful witness
    My Christmas gift is a powerful
  Powerful witness before the Lord

26

GOOD BY TO YOUR SPIRIT

The Lord shall prepare my life n you for
Me to be blessing in the Christmas day
    Of holiness
  Good-by to your spirit
I receiver a nice gift of love in the
Christmas wise of the Holy Ghost
    From heaven
     Good-by to your spirit
Your Christmas spirit shall prevail in
My soul for ever with a moment of
  Peace in the holy city of Bethlehem
     Good-by to your spirit
One day your spirit shall be a Christmas
Blessing to someone in the world of
Wisdom for a Christmas peace to you
      In holiness

27

MISTLETOES IN CHRISTMAS

My salvation is common upon the branch
   Of praise in the mistletoes of Christmas
      The mistletoes of Christmas are a shine
   Star that light up the world for the wise
   Men to go into Bethlehem to see the
            New baby
         Mistletoes in Christmas
The Lord known my life are weary some
Time in this old world of Christmas that
Wanted faint in his presence of his living
Prayer   mistletoes in Christmas

28

DWELLS IN CHRISTMAS

A long line of the congregation was waiting
  For the present spirit of the Holy Savior to
  Came into the Holy City with peace as
Their dwells in the Christmas grace
      Dwells in Christmas
A soft voice went out to preacher the
Gospel for the congregation
    Dwells in Christmas
According to Christmas for the holiness in
  The gospel field went out to be praise in the
      The preacher words
      Dwells in Christmas

29

A SPECIAL CHRISTMAS

I was healed according to the love in the
Spirit of Christmas as a gift to the world
With peace in my heart
A special Christmas
God have a special gift for everyone with
His blessing to you on Christmas day
A special Christmas
The prophet came into the temple with a
Passover for a gift in the field of paradise
For Christmas
A special Christmas

30

PEACE IN CHRISTMAS

Go out and preaching for peace in your
Christmas miracle to someone that are
In happy with their life
Peace in Christmas
You can help someone in the spirit of grace
In the justified power of your Christmas
Miracle
Peace in Christmas
Peace in your blessing

31

HOLY POWER

I ministered to the saints in judgment
On the battle field with the holy angels
Standing under the Christmas tree
    Holy power, Holy Christmas
Holy power came together in a dwell
  Mercy as you look to heaven with
All the saints on the battle field
Holy power, Holy Christmas

32

WE WAITED

As I waited for Santa in the holy city of
Bethlehem with wisdom on Christmas
Night   We waited we waited
We shall wait on Christmas to come
    Into our lives when the holy shepherd
        Came out the field of salvation so we
Can see the new baby in Bethlehem
            We waited we waited
Jesus are the Savior of Christmas for
The world be at peace in their soul as
    You waited for him in the Christmas
        Season We waited we waited

33

FIVE DEACONS

A crossed rise's in someone heart when
  Their walked in faiths of the five deacons to
Bright up the Christmas tree in the center
Of your heart
    Five deacons came and look up to
    Heaven to see the wise men standing around
      The Christmas tree with the angels of holiness
        Five deacons and six holy deacons

34

MY COVENANT

Beware of the devil due this holy season with
Wisdom that came in to someone soul but the
Lord voice shall carry you to his cross
The covenant shall carry you into this Christmas
Holiday season with your life in the Lord holy hand
                    Of peace
My covenant shall come to you with a
        Miracle of Christmas
My covenant my covenant

35

GOLDEN CHRISTMAS

Comforter of your Christmas gift shall come
To you in a drop of rain dust from out of the
Air in happiness due to you in his faith
       Golden Christmas
Who ever come in form of angel and your
Golden Christmas shall bring you peace
In your heart from heaven one day
       Golden Christmas
I'm not afraid to step out of the shadow
For the Lord golden Christmas so all of
Us can see the bright star that shine
 Down on the world

36

THREE HUNDERD CHRISTMAS STARS

A stranger proceeded to the problem land
In a three years march toward the Christmas
       Spirit
       Three hundred Christmas stars
Christmas creep up on my dears love one in
Worship for the saints in a difference town
       Of Zion
       Three hundred Christmas stars
On my way to Golden town of Zion I saw
Three hundred stars on a big Christmas
Tree shining bright around the town of
       Holiness

37

DEFILED NOT IN THE SPIRIT

Defiled not the spirt of the Lord beloved
Power in prayer of Christmas for you
Defiled not in the spirit
    Defiled in the clean power of holiness
        For your flesh to be blessing in the
          Living God praise of faith in the
            Christmas joy pf prayer that came
            Into your heart with grace of the
            Living God Christmas

38

SEEING IN THE CHRISTMAS DROPS

I shall understand the drops of my righteousness
Christmas tears of summer to be clean by all
Manner from Christmas seeing in the Christmas
                    Drops
My grace is in the unjust time of a Christmas
Drops of rain that fall from the holy season of
                    Christmas
Seeing in the Christmas drops of the holiday with
Your blessing that came down from heaven
         Seeing in the Christmas drops

39

IN THE HOLY LAND

Be of a good honor with the holiness in
The holy land of Christmas for you in the
Lord salvation
    In the holy land of wisdom
My life is strong in the face of the Lord
Christmas miracle for me one day as I prayer
    For my salvation in the Lord of judgment
        In the holy land of joy
          In the holy land of praise
            In Christmas

40

FEARED OF CHRISTMAS

I weep for a blessing to come inform
Me of Christmas gift in the vineyard
　　　Fear of Christmas
The promise of God shall come into
　　Your soul as you fear the Christmas
　　　Blessing in a moment of time that
　　　　You have in your heart
　　　　　Fear of Christmas

41

THE DEW

Your glory is the everlasting praise of
　　Christmas when your tear reached
　　　　Up to heaven in a tiny voice of
　　　　　　Peace
　　　　　　　The dew of time
　　　　　　　　The dew of wisdom
Verily I shall come to you in a dance of life
　　For you to show me your light around the
Shine Christmas prayer in the pure tree of
　　　　　　　A moment
　　　　　　The dew of happiness
　　　　　　　The dew of love

42

A CHRISTMAS IN THE WILDERNESS

You shall dwell in the rising sun of a Christmas
With a pure heart for the congregation in the
Wilderness of life for you
A Christmas in the wilderness
My season blessing will come into my life
With a give hand in holiness of praise
For the Lord in the kingdom
A Christmas in the wilderness
My love will not perish for the Christmas
Everlasting faith that I hold in my heart
For the holy heart for the holy season
A Christmas in the wilderness

43

THE SHADOW

God shadow came up behind me in the
    Christmas spirit of grace
   The shadow of love
Some time my mind go back on the time
We spend together in the past Christmas
       Season
     The shadow in peace
Whoso ever reach the hill in light up the
Moment of their life with a tiny Christmas
   Miracle will come their way
    The shadow of salvation

44

UPON THE CHRISTMAS

I enter in a Christmas door of paradise to
Descended in the light of the pure city
    With the shepherd
    Upon the Christmas
The power of Christmas wish can be seen
Around the holy town of faith
    Upon the Christmas
Lord sent down a tiny promise for everyone
    To come into the Christmas prayer to
      Be full a blessing
    Upon the Christmas

45

MANIFESTED

I shall keep the promise in my life as
I go down the path to the Christmas
City with your holy angels in Bethlehem
   Manifested to the world to come
         Together
One day I will rise to see the Christmas
Tree and be a witness to the new baby that
Came into world to live in so many life with
His holy hand to hold you today
    Manifested to the world to come
       Together

46

RAISED UP CHRISTMAS

I am omega of Christmas in your path way
To bear the holy praise in the temple of
        Grace
     Raised up Christmas
I am the life in the Christmas mercy of a
Newness prater before the shepherd on
     The battle fielded
     Raised up Christmas
I believed in my heart for a little blessing
That are come my way one day soon
     Raised up Christmas

47

MY BLOOD

M blood endure the love in the Christmas
Light to shine down on the salvation in a
         Small voice
My blood is in the Christmas fountain
         Of omega
My wage of Christmas peace come out of
My voice when I prayer in the spirit for
Someone to show me the right path to mind
         Way in a miracle
My holy blood come out of a powerful
Christmas from heaven with the shepherd

48

MY LIFE ARE CHAINS OF PEACE

I heard a tiny voice coming from out
     Of the wind
My life is a chain of peace that will not
Perish in form of a Christmas paradise
   Let all the Christmas come together
For everyone in the spirit and the love
     Of Christmas
  My life is a chain of Christmas
I have the love of Christmas spirit in mind
Heart for the world and for the holy grace
    In your heart

49

GIVE A HOLY CHRISTMAS

The Lord call for the elf to come and spread
Out his gift to everyone for a Christmas
Fountain to fill your soul with his holy
      Praise
The Lord lift the power in his hand
Of faith in a Christmas paradise that are
    In their heart everyday
Give a holy Christmas to shine around
The world in praise for the Savior
      Give a holy Christmas

50

NEWNESS IN THE SPIRIT

All gladness come inform of the
Newness of a brands new Christmas gift
   For the Savior
In due time of newness of your faith
In the Christmas church to overcome
    The pain of happiness
      Newness in the spirit
My newness of a Christmas echo in mind
Soul for the lost my love one's that
Live in my life and for the Savior of the
     World in the spirit

51

I NEED A LITTLE BLESSING

I need a little blessing in my heart for a
Christmas miracle to be full the grace
   In holiness and the center of my soul
      I need a little blessing
My Christmas spirit shall not raise up
For the world judgment that are full of
Love for me to see the mean of a Christmas
Blessing   I need a little blessing

52

MY PROMISE

The light of a promise Christmas is my secret
Of the Lord holy hand full of wisdom in someone
Life as they go into the temple to kneel and
    Prayer and seal up their Christmas gift
        My promise is love
Whoso even show everlasting peace for the
Grace of Christmas in their life
    My promise love is in the open air of
Heaven when the shepherd came out of the field
        In a Christmas blessing
    My promise my promise in the secret part of a
        Christmas miracle in my heart

53

WHO LOVE ME

My flesh can command peace in the
Christmas of holiness that came out
Of pure salvation in the wind of heaven
      Who love me
I overcome the track of a moment to
Live in the power of the Holy Ghost
      Who love me
I deliver in the Christmas faith and in
The Lord who love me

54

THE LATTER RAIN

In the open air of Christmas God shall
Bring he gift of holiness into your life
With a miracle of hope for the latter
      Rain of a moment
In the latter rain God love shine in
Your heart for a Christmas miracle
That shine in rose star of glory from
The holy land of a Christmas latter rain

55

A SPECIAL HOLY CHRISTMAS

I heard a small voice behind me in a special
Holiday of the Christmas season for me to
Look forth in my soul for peace
      A special Holy Christmas
In a way I stand on the land in the holy city
Of Bethlehem when the Lord light's up mind
       Way to his temple in grace
   A special holy Christmas
    A special holy season

56

DEPART INTO A HOLY TEMPLE

Enforce the dark light of time to shine
In the Christmas moment for the Savior
    Depart into a holy temple
Early in worship the saints came into
A lighting wood to see a holy temple
Of faith on Christmas morning
    Depart into a holy temple
A king departed into a holy temple with a
Christmas word for you in the spirit of God

57

PRECIOUS CHRISTMAS

The angel restored her faith in the
Holy spirit of salvation when her saw
A precious Christmas star in the vine
      Yard
        Precious Christmas
I appeal my faith to the Lord in prayer for
A Christmas blessing to come into my life
In a perfect way as I walk in his light of
          Holiness
Precious Christmas precious praise

58

GOD REPLACE

I travel to the holy city of Bethlehem to
See the new baby when I cast my life
Upon God bosoms in prayer
God replace my light on his Christmas
Tree for the wise men to follow the shining
Star to Bethlehem

God replace this wick world into a
Blessing of peace for everyone to become
Clean under the Christmas star

59

DWELLED UNDER THE CHRISTMAS STAR

The rod was a Christmas star for the
Different among the angels and shepherds
     In a stranger city
  Dwelled under the Christmas star
I receiver the power of love in a moment
For the Christmas star to brighten up the
     Spirit in your heart
  Dwelled under the Christmas star
The command from heaven came down in
The spirit of a holy fire that burn all round
The holy angel of the living God as a Christmas
Gift to the church of prayer
  Dwelled under the Christmas star

60

THE HOLY MANGER

My heart is in the Christmas moment with
Prayer and I have a silver star to shine
          Around the holy manger
                The holy manger
The Savior was wrapping in swaddling
Clothes were the wise men follow the
Star to the holy city for the Christmas
                Season
          The holy manger
The shine light to shone in the Christmas
     Spirit of heaven with the shepherds in
          The field of glory
                The holy manger

61

PRAISE CHRISTMAS

Let your tender mercy came in
The Christmas of prayer of your
        Heart
      Praise Christmas
In the Christmas spirit a trumpet
Were blew in the center of Zion
For the gift from the holiness of
     Peace in your heart
       Praise Christmas
Let your blessing be for a gift in the
Christmas king grace to come forth
     In prayer
    Praise Christmas

62

THE CAVE OF CHRISTMAS

Upon a wide table by the power
In your soul where are a Christmas
        Bible
    The cave of Christmas
Enjoy came out of a Christmas miracle
Of praise among the angels in the
    Town of holiness for your happiness
      The cave of Christmas

63

BITTERLY CHRISTMAS

I reign in a happy way with a wonderful
Holiday are not a bitterly Christmas to
Have in your life please be joyful for
  This season in holiness
   Bitterly Christmas
The Savior live in your heart for the
Holiday season so you can enjoy your
   Life in the spirit
  Bitterly Christmas
I stood in the line of wisdom for someone
To be happy for this Christmas season and
   Not bitterly
  Bitterly Christmas

64

RED BLUE CHRISTMAS

I bowed down low under the star of
Victory as the Lord celebrate the
Precious season that reign in the
Red blue Christmas holiday
    Red blue Christmas
I departed by the power of a Christmas
Miracle from heaven in the Lord hand
      Of victory
    Red blue Christmas
The Lord tie a bright red and blue
Ribbon around the Christmas tree
In Bethlehem for the wise men to
Celebrate the love of Christmas
     In their life
    Red blue Christmas

65

HE STRETCHED

The holy angel stretched out the
Light among the shepherd around
The praise in the vineyard on Christmas
     City of holiness
     He stretched, stretched
I redeem in the spirit of Christmas and
I shall rise by the power of the Lord
     Grace
     He stretched, stretched
Let me kneel under the Christmas
Tree with the holy saints for the
     Season in heaven
He stretched, stretched

66

THE SEASON IN CHRISTMAS

I fear not the faith upon a everlasting
Stone of wisdom in the season of
      Christmas
I went up to the top of the hill with a
Christmas blessing for everyone to
Hear the holy word in the season of
       Christmas
My life is in the hand of the Lord
As he comforted my soul in his Christmas
        Wisdom
In the season of Christmas there is a blessing
  For you in the Lord kingdom

67

THE BIBLE IN CHRISTMAS

A deacon holds the bible in his life
For a blessing in Christmas
The bible in Christmas
I stand up in the spirit of a Christmas
Dance of the spoken word of the
Lord
The bible in Christmas
In the deacon heart there was a
Tiny vessel with a holy gift full of
Christmas blessing
The bible in Christmas

68

RETURNED TO CHRISTMAS

I have a new testament in my life
   For the grace of the Lord in
      Christmas
   Returned to Christmas
There is a teacher live in my soul
For the victory in the Christmas
   Holy city
   Returned to Christmas
My dust is in the shadow of
Salvation that are a part of mind
Christmas miracle that the Lord
Returned to me in the spirit of
   My soul
   Returned to Christmas

69

A KNOWLEDGE CHRISTMAS

In order of a darkness moon I shall follow
A comfort shadow to the temple of
        Christmas
     A knowledge Christmas
In a few day my holy spirit shall rise
Up toward the kingdom with my life
In the palm of the Lord with a comfort
Shadow reach to heaven in one day
Of my life with a miracle Christmas
     A knowledge Christmas
My order in a Christmas praise is in my
Payer of the shadow and a peace offering s
Season when the Christmas angel that come
To me from the holy temple of the Lord
     A knowledge Christmas

70

HOLLY STAR CHRISTMAS

A whirlwind raised up the sleeping
Saints in the land of Christmas to be
      Holy
  Holly star Christmas
The star of Christmas came into
The world to fill your faith in everyone
     Soul at a gift to God
    Holly star Christmas
Your gift of holiness came in the whirlwind
Of a Christmas gift before the sleeping
    Saints upon a star in Christmas
      Holly star Christmas

71

BEHOLD YOUR ANSWERED

God impact my vision in peace for me to
Perform in his Christmas gift play in the
          Wilderness
          Behold your answered
I was influence by the grace in my life to
Celebration the love of wisdom upon a
Christmas star that shine on Bethlehem
          Behold your answered
God sent down a golden star to shine
Upon my Christmas gift in Bethlehem
          For me
          Behold your answered

72

BRAND NEW CHRISTMAS PRESENT

The might angel reign among the saint in a
In brand new Christmas spirit on the second
Day of their life
Brand new Christmas present
I have a tiny plan that went upon a high
Hill in a thousand time on Christmas with
A blessing for you in the holy spirit of
Service in your life

73

CHRISTMAS FRIENDS

We worship the holy season of holiness
That ascend into the sky on Christmas
For our friends in a miracle of happiness
That flow down into the temple
Christmas friends
A Christmas friend yield to the holy
Angel for you to come into his great
Power of peace in your life with the
Lord grace in a Christmas wisdom

74

COVER ME IN A CHRISTMAS GIFT

THE Lord command his root in your life
To be cover in your gift for Christmas
    Cover me in a Christmas gift
My tender mercies are to cover up in a
Moment of joy for me to be in his precious
       Blood of salvation
   Cover me in a Christmas gift
The Lord show up to under cover your gift
In his holiness of peace when the shepherd
Came out of the field when he receiver
    Your gift for a Christmas present to them
   Cover me in a Christmas gift

75

MY KINGDOM

God cast out a long line for you to
Catch in time of sad that came into
      Your heart
        My kingdom
My dominion is discovered by the
Powerful of decree of my love in God
Kingdom as a gift in his Christmas praise
           Of victory
             My kingdom
God shall show me a tiny gift of
Peace on Christmas morning for
Me to be strong in his faith
        My kingdom

76

BEHOLD MY FAITH

The fear came dance in the temple
For me behold my faith in a sign of
Prayer that march upon a little
Christmas star that shine in Bethlehem
    Behold my faith
The fear of happiness came at a moment
When I needed someone to praise Christmas
Time in my life when the saints was singing a
Hymn of glory for a praise offering in the temple
           On Christmas
  Behold my faith in a tiny place of Christmas

77

CLOUDS OF HEAVEN

In my morning vision that pass near
To my pain in the life with a little grief
Of sadness time that enter in the wind
Of time that dwell in someone soul
With love
Clouds of heaven is a shadow that
Follow you in to Christmas season of
Praise
My Christmas present went up into the
Air with the holy saints of Bethlehem
Clouds of heaven
Clouds of peace
Clouds of Christmas

78

FOUR WINDS IN CHRISTMAS

I hear a soft sound of Christmas music
Coming down for you to celebrate
    The season from heaven
Four winds in Christmas
I believer in the spirit of the four
Winds in the Christmas power as you
Prayer before the holy baby in the
       Holy city
Four winds in Christmas
The four winds in Christmas dream
Came out of your season of holiness
  Four winds in Christmas

79

I WROTE IN MY CHRISTMAS SEASON

I strove up to my season in the
Christmas faith in my heart for the
Everlasting hymn to serve in the
                Wisdom
I wrote in my Christmas season
    I wrote a little note for my gift
In the Christmas season when I open
Up my book in the season of Christmas
I wrote in my Christmas season for you
To encourage someone to come into the
Lord church for a tiny blessing as a gift
In the precious spirit of Christmas miracle
For your love one by the holy power in
                Your life
I wrote in my Christmas season

80

YOUR DREAM CHRISTMAS

God choose the shepherd for his present
In the dream of a great victory of Christmas
     Your dream Christmas
He plucked up a tree to celebrate his gift
To the Church around the world when
The angles gather to restore the congregation
    In his faith of a paradise on Christmas
        Your dream Christmas

81

GO THY WAY

I shall go my way to enter in
The Christmas spirit of the
                Season
            Go thy way
On Christmas morning I went into
The synagogue to prayer for the world
To come together by the power in the
            Lord   Go thy way
I shall dwell in the Christmas season
Of holiness that you cast your gift to
            Someone in victory
            Go thy way
    I shall go my way to see the
Christmas light that shine in Zion

82

ENTER NO MORE

JESUS sent out a gift card for the
Christmas grace in your life
       Enter no more
I saw a small child set by big
Christmas tree and he was very
Happy to see the light shine
Around the holy city of Bethlehem
     Enter no more
I enter no more into the classical
Land of Christmas as a little baby
   Born under the mistletoe
      Enter no more

83

A PEACEFUL CHRISTMAS

I exclusive a gift in paradise for the
Unbelief as the shepherd come into
A peaceful Christmas season's
      A peaceful Christmas
I heard rumors in the mistletoe holiday
Of retail freedom that appeared in my soul
For a little while on Christmas
      A peaceful Christmas
The shepherds were looking for the
Holy season and the star shall shine
In the glory of salvation for a moment
      In the church with the Lord
      A peaceful Christmas

84

I LOOKED AROUND

God collection a present for his baby
Jesus in the holy land with a changed
That dance in the spirit of his amaze
　　　Word in the channel of faith
　　　　I looked around
Some moment of Christmas I looked
Around and I saw a little angel handed
The world a gift of grace in a vessel of
　　　Love to them
　　　　I looked around
God collected a pray for you to fasting
In the season of Christmas

85

TWO VESSELS IN THE SEASON

In the time of God full my two vessels in
His season for the children to receiver their
      Gifts in the Christmas spirit
      Two vessels in the season
The cloud hangs down for a gift on Christmas
Day to lead you into a shadow for them to
      Listen to a voice in the holy season
      Two vessels in the season
God can send out a present in his love for
The world to come together in the Christmas
      Season of wisdom
      Two vessels in the season

86

IN THE MIDST OF CHRISTMAS

My grace is awesome in a midst of
Christmas blessing for the little ones
    In a midst of Christmas
My Christmas power transfigured right
Before the church in the platform when
God planting his ministry in my life on
      Christmas
    In a midst of Christmas

87

A MISLETOE ANSWERED

Peter answered the Christmas voice in
His amazed peace offering before the
   Lord
 A mistletoe answered
God protect your soul in his Christmas
   Season of holiness
Someone in the precious season went with
Out in peace to preach to the congregation
On Christmas morning in the temple
   A mistletoe answered
I shall remain in the blessing of a mistletoe
Christmas in my answered that came out
 Of my heart for a gift to the new baby
   A mistletoe Christmas

88

IN HIS SALVATION

My Christmas power comfort the everlasting
      Battle in the worship of wisdom
          In his salvation
In his Christmas salvation I shall come out
    Of my shadow in a power of his glory
          In his salvation
I shall hold a tiny seed in my heart that came
Out of the shadow in the mistletoe Christmas
        Of prayer
        In his salvation
My voice will receiver a soft word as a gift
On Christmas night when the angle come
      Into the season of happiness
        In his salvation

89

THE STRONG SAINT

I rose up to the strong faith in the
Might wind of praise in my Christmas
Miracle that dwell in the gate of holiness
      The strong saint
My fire burned in the strong flame of
Christmas for the saint to hold onto
   My gift in the miracle of praise
       The strong saint
Someone turned my gift into a strong
Shadow of wisdom for my Christmas
   Blessing from God
     The strong saint

90

DRAWS BACK'

I shall not prevail my spirit in the
Cast of Christmas when the Lord
Draws back his gift to comforter
You in the holiness of his happiness
    Draws back draws back
A great victory rest in your lift with the
Chief of holiness to fill your Christmas
    Vessel with his love for you
    Draws back draws back
Your beat is in his Christmas prayer
That coming out of your door in a
     Hymn of victory
  Draws back draws back
I will not draw back my tears of happiness in a
blessing for a gift in a Christmas praise for you

91

RELIEVE YOUR BLESSING

One day I will swallow up the wicked
That Satan cast down into my life with the
Praise at the well of salvation in a moment
Of his holy praise in the Christmas vessel
       Of peace
Relieve your blessing
     Relieve your Christmas gift into
       The church with a blessing

92

SANCTUARY CHRISTMAS

God cover Zion in a sanctuary Christmas
Miracle that came dancing in the moon
Light of peace with his precious angels
   Of heaven
  Sanctuary Christmas
A beauty moment that came up in your
Sanctuary Christmas peace offering that
Block my tears out of my life with a present
  For everyone
  Sanctuary Christmas

93

RECEIVER A PRECIOUS GIFT

God send out his angels to preacher a
Good word in the wilderness on
Christmas
Receiver a precious gift
My gift is precious on a Christmas night
For the angels to celebration his grace
On a new holiday of glory that came into
The holy season of wisdom that flow down
The high point in a Christmas salvation

94

A GOOD CROSS

The rubies cross over into a Christmas
Nobel of peace with the holy prayer
That came to honor the shepherd in
     The high mountain
   A good cross a good book
I shall reign in the good cross according to
My faith in a Christmas blessing of holiness
   A good cross a good book
My Christmas vision is a little word that
The Lord send down from heaven with
His holy angels in the spirit of holiness
   A good cross a good book

95

HIS HOLY SON

The king sent out a helping gift to his
Holy son in a Christmas miracle in twenty
Ways for you to be again to praise his power
Under the Christmas tree that dwell in the
       Wilderness of victory in him
  His holy son your holy child
I reign on Christmas night in a field of
Peace before his holy son in Bethlehem
With peace in my heart for his little
Children in the season of paradise on
        Christmas
His holy son his holy children
   His holy son his holy children

96

COMMAND CHRISTMAS

My command came in peace to the supplication
Of his judgment on the command of his Christmas
In faith to worship him in my life
        Command Christmas
My testimony is a command Christmas in a
Vessel of rejoicing for me to speak with mind
Soul to keeper his season of holiness in the
        Church
        Command Christmas
My command came down and behold my life in
The wisdom of Christmas praise that enter the
Holiday of prayer for you to be holies
        Command Christmas

97

ACCORDING TO HIM

I suffer no judgment according to his broken
Peace on the Christmas cross when the star
Shine in your soul that rose up in the air
   According to him
Someday I shall utter a Christmas cry in the
Wilderness of praise for my salvation in the
Temple of praise before the Lord spirit
   According to him

98

AMONG THE CHRISTGMAS SPIRIT

My cheeks are a vessel in the honor of a Christmas
Cross that cover in the holiness of my love in
      Heaven
       Among the Christmas spirit
I depart into a running crush faith of the
Minister with the angels that fall from heaven
     On Christmas morning
   Among the Christmas spirit
I receiver a Christmas power for a gift from
Heaven in the Lord precious moment of
     His holiness
   Among the Christmas spirit

99

REPENTED IN THE CHRISTMAS

God justified my receiver law as a dance
Under the Christmas tree for his disciples
To be blessing by his prayer in the holy
       Land of peace
         Repented in the Christmas
God influenced his preacher power to come up
Out the dust of time for you to be a gift in his grace
          Of hid victory on Christmas
       Repented in the Christmas
Someday I shall repent in his Christmas power

In mind life when I dance under his shadow of
          Holiness
     Repented in the Christmas

100

APPEARD IN PARADISE

I celebrate in his paradise of salvation on
Christmas road of the kingdom with a little
Shine star that never go out in his season of
       His wisdom for you
       Appear in paradise
Appear in his miracle door of Christmas
As a witness for the congregation in his
       Temple of heaven
       Appear in a Christmas walking in my life
And in his holy land of victory come for his glory
       In my heart of pray

101

CAME INTO A CHRISTMAS CITY

I have a sackcloth full of present for the
Poor in the answered of the Christmas city
    In the wilderness
      Came into a Christmas city
I enter a Christmas city with his
Precious saints to receiver my gift from
The holy angels of peace in my soul
      Came into a Christmas city

102

ANOINTING CHRISTMAS GIFTS

Jesus sent out his shepherds to preacher
The word for anointing Christmas so the
Blind could see their blessing in his spirit
    Of the gospel in the world
     Anointing Christmas city
He came down and heal their broken heart
In his anointed power as a gift of a miracle
For them to see his Christmas tree in the
     Holy land of grace
    Anointing Christmas City
He shall anoint my Christmas gift with
His peace offering in my heart
    Anointing Christmas City

103

TWENTY SIXTH SOUL

In the church was full of grief lost soul
Went up in the spirit of heaven to be
With the Lord when someone came in
Shouting with a heavy soul full and the
    Wicked spirit
    Twenty sixth souls
Some start to run and hiding behind
A desk and dash under a chair for they
Life as the gun man enter the church
With a gun in his hand and before he
Stop shooting he at killing twenty sixth
      Souls
    Twenty sixth souls
      Twenty sixth souls went home to be with
         The Lord

104

INCLUDING IN THE WHITE BELL

I look out over the crown in the
Season of a bell ringing in the sound
Of a Christmas train come in the power
  Of a white bell of the holiday
  Including in the white bell
My Christmas bell are including
To comfort the everlasting prayer
In someone life when there are
Dance under the shine star in the
Precious temple of your spirit in
          Christmas
  Including in the white bell

105

A CHRISTMAS KEY IN HEAVEN

Losing my classics key to heaven when the
Angel appeared before the golden Christmas
Of the season when their gift are a blessing
    In their heart
   A Christmas key in heaven
You can be lifted heaven when you
Unlock the door to your Christmas gift
From the Lord with your spirit that in you
  A Christmas key in heaven
The Lord have my Christmas key for me
To enter his holiday season of heaven
      A Christmas key in heaven

106

DELIGHT MISTLETOE

Teacher in the knowledge of a Christmas
Miracle come into the delight of a mistletoe
In the holy salvation of peace to the season
      Of happiness
    Delight mistletoe
My holy Christmas mistletoe shall not be
Moved in the prayer blessing of paradise
      Delight mistletoe
I shall form my Christmas power in the
Holy rock of joy that carried my soul in
    The holy city of wisdom

107

WORSHIP THE HOLY HOLIDAY

The Lord came and ministered to his angles
In the worship on his holiday season for a
    Gift on Christmas morning
The Lord sent out the shepherd to see
The true holiness in the season of his
Christmas blessing for the world
    Worship the holy holiday
He choose the vision of a big
Christmas tree in a worship serve
    Of the wilderness
    Worship the holy holiday

108

A CHRISTMAS TREE STAND

Peace was cast into someone heart for
His glory to be blessing them in the
Opening faith of wisdom in heaven for
A gift to them on Christmas day
     A Christmas tree stand
My life was bound upon a shining a new
Moon as the Lord touched my heart on
       Christmas day
    A Christmas tree stand
A soft whisper came under the barren spirit
Of a gift hanging on a Christmas tree of faith
That press on a crown in the paradise of peace
      A Christmas tree stand

109

A VIRGIN IN CHRISTMAS HOLINESS

The virgin was a angel in a gift of the
Lord Christmas to the answered in the
       Holy ministered of victory
      A virgin in Christmas holiness
I behold my faith in the door of heaven
That came down in a rain drop that fall
Into my heart on Christmas
      A virgin in Christmas holiness
No hurt come up from the holy temple of
Peace on Christmas morning for me to
Conceiver the power in the spirit of wisdom
Upon a star in the season of peace
    A virgin in Christmas holiness

110

THE CHRISTMAS PRISONS

The Lord phone his angels in heaven
To come and appeared as a present
In the Christmas prison of salvation
    The Christmas prisons
My life is a river bed full of the Lord
Ministered of grace that bear the golden
Cross in the kingdom of his victory
    The Christmas prisons
One Christmas night the Lord open up
The door to the prison of my soul for me
To be at peace in holiness of the church
     On Christmas
    The Christmas prisons

111

ON THE NINTH HOUR OF CHRISTMAS

The flock of holy saints are look on the
Ninth hour to behold a dream in the season
Of the wide open in the Christmas air that
Touch your heart in the ninth hour of holiness
    On the ninth hour of Christmas
I stood under the saints that was beating the
Drum in my heart on the ninth hour of Christmas
      On the ninth hour of Christmas
The holy power went out fly around the Christmas
Tree with the angels in heaven as their prayer in
      The spirit with the saints
    On the ninth hour of Christmas

112

CHRISTMAS IS KNOCKED

Christmas is knocked in your gift for the
Little children who are watch out for
Santa in a special way in Bethlehem
       Christmas is knocked
My miracle came knocked to celebrate
The baking cooking of praise in the season
That are knocked in the church with a whisper
         Of peace
       Christmas is knocked

113

FEAR THE FEEL IN MY HEART

A classics name was the midst of a
Dream in the minister of Christmas
    Fear the feel in my heart
My glory was a mouth piece for the Christmas
Gift of time that ring upon the miracle moon of a
Christmas tree that grown toward heaven in the
Holy season for you to be at peace on Christmas
        Morning
  Fear the feel in my heart
    Feared came down on the star
      Of Christmas in the holy season
        With the little baby of Bethlehem
        Fear the feel in my heart

114

SUNRISE CHRISTMAS

The wonderful place was not a weeping victory
Of snow to fall from a deep moment of your
                    Soul
            Sunrise Christmas
I respected the Lord holiness when the sunrise
On the Christmas cross of victory to turn mind
Perfect way toward heaven with his shepherd
On his battlefield of happiness in a Christmas
                    Peace of praise
Sunrise Christmas
    Sunrise Christmas is in your
        Member of joy on Christmas day

115

MY SOUL IS FULL OF CHRISTMAS

Erred in the sacrifices of holiness of my blessing
That came down in the spirit of Christmas so mind
Life can be a miracle I prayer in heaven
    My soul is full of Christmas
I wanted provoked anyone into the Satan power
Because they life are with the Lord In heaven so I
Living in the power of the Christmas spirit
  My soul is full of Christmas
    My gift is a part of my life
      In the Lord salvation

116

AN APOSTLE CHRISTMAS

I heard a prayer of rightness in a major
Pass on the road of a apostle Christmas
Wish of your religion in the church
    of Christmas wisdom
     An apostle Christmas
I was set by the Red River with the precious angel
From the gospel as a witness in the Christmas
        Grace
   An apostle Christmas
    An apostle had a foundation
     In the church of living in peace for
      God salvation in the vineyard of freedom
      An apostle Christmas

117

THE CHIEF ANGEL

The chief angel gathered the elders of the Christmas
Victory to come and speak to the congregation
In the hold season of paradise to be a pointed
To the Lord ministry of labor in his temple
    Of wisdom
   The chief angel
I glorified the chief angel on Christmas
To be a built in their soul for the foundation
Of Jesus glory every moment as a gift to the
    World on Christmas
   The chief angel

118

READY CHRISTMAS

Someone are a partaker of the Holy Ghost
On the ready Christmas minister in faith
When the Lord sent you to preacher to
His saints in the gospel field of holiness
     On Christmas
     Ready Christmas
I shall worship in his temple of teacher
Someday by his glory when the word
Come down and enter the holy
Spirit of a blessing on Christmas
     Ready Christmas
      Ready Christmas

119

I THANK YOU FOR THE HOLY WORD

I survive a blameless Christmas power in the
Holy word of fasted before the purchase upon
    A high tree in the wilderness
        I thank you for the holy word
I shall not prevail against the Christmas
Miracle in my good faith in the presence
Of the Holy Ghost when the angel lighted up
      The Christmas tree in heaven
  I thank you for the holy word

120

REPORTED CHRISTMAS

God looser the short rope to his reported in
Christmas for the member of his congregation
In the holiness of a miracle that came in out of
The world to see his Christmas star in the air
    Reported Christmas reported a blessing
God reported my Christmas stone for me to
Stand on among his shepherd in his vineyard
              Of wisdom
  Reported Christmas reported blessing
My reported are a Christmas to clean his
Precious shade of glory with a soft voice
From heaven for you to bare the crown
          Of peace

121

GOD REIGNED ON CHRISTMAS

My glad tiding is hung on the Christmas
Of peace to become clean as a tree of a
Holy star that fear the power in your soul
To be hold in the arms of Jesus
    God reigned on Christmas
My glory in revealed in the grown beauty
Moment in a Christmas seed of sorrow bruised
Victory are a part of my honor on the floor in
          Peace
   God reigned on Christmas
I reigned in the vessel to proclaim my voice
On Christmas day to root out my tears in the
     Little moment of freedom
       God reigned on Christmas

122

A STAR DEAL FOR CHRISTMAS

In the great of labored I turned my face to the wall
And prayer in the time of a healed unclean the
      Spirit of Christmas
    A star deal for Christmas
Knowledge justify stripes you down in the
Christmas gospel that wounded your life
In heaven with the angels of grace
    A star deal for Christmas
The vessel is fill of gifts from the Lord
Christmas shepherd in a good soul of
Peace that fall into Zion
A star deal for Christmas

123

OPENED UP

Poured out of your holy life so the Lord
Can fill the grief heart with his Christmas
Present so you can be happy again
   Opened up
I rejected a tender comforted in the air
With the labored of hope in the season of
Christmas for the world to come together
      In the Lord salvation
Opened your heart
   Opened your soul
     Opened your Christmas present
       To the world for peace in your life

124

STRONG FEELING

I continue to be strong with my feel in a
Proud Christmas faith of understand that
Surround me in the Holy Spirit
Strong feel strong power
My soul is prepared for the question of a
Rage pray of praise in the Christmas blast
Of the holy blood
Strong feel strong power
My shadow is in the white pasture with mind
My feel for the Christmas shepherd on this path
Of judgment for your life to beat peace in this season
Strong feel strong power

125

ACCORDING TO YOUR CHRISTMAS BLESSING

Come and gather up the princes of honor
To shout for victory in the dry land when
You are weep for a gift in the spoken word
      On Christmas
   According to your Christmas blessing
I yielded up my miracle for a great called in a
Christmas testimony that came out of the
      Dust of your heart
   According to your Christmas blessing

126

A SOUND IN THE HOLY CITY

I bear the command of the sound upon
The cross with a bishop that ruler his saints
In the spirit
A sound in the holy city
My soul went straight up into the Christmas
Air as I wept for his happiness to enter the
World with a moment of Christmas miracle
That rise in the holy season of holiness
A sound in the holy city

HOLY SALVATION

BY LILLIE MAE HIPPS DICKERSON

Gene enter the Holy Salvation of a dream in faith to playing in a
Brief moment of the temple. As he looked for a blessing every where
With a might spirit that came out of his heart as he prayer for peace
With his family in holiness to create a strong power in the world
An old friend pops up out the wind of time to be close to him as he
Went through hard time after he lose someone close to him
He was very sad for a long time and no one could show him the
Happy way to live his life for a long time so he journeys a long time
In the holy salvation to fine the means of God in his life
One day God came into his life with love for him to see his way to the
Church to service him in the precious spirit of the Holy Ghost
Your spirit is not finish with a blessing that came out of your soul
For the Lord I shall ring out a holy bell to the world in my love with
All the saints in the wilderness
A space in his life are empty for him to love someone in his faith and
In prayer but some day he shall be happy again by the power in God
Victory that the Lord have for him in the grace of the church in Zion
So Gene would follow him into the Holy Land of salvation with holy
Angel when he shouted for joy as you waited for a moment of peace
To come before him in the temple with the judgment that came before
You and in h

is life as you journey down this road with him in your life
Gene glorify the spirit and his soul was lifted to heaven at
He journeys- into the temple and he was fill with the wisdom
Of grace that came into his life with Holy Ghost
I spoken to his little sister Jean by the power in a good word

From the Living God of holiness
My soul enters the garden of praise with the victory of faith
That came into Gene heart as he prayer for peace to come
To him some day in judgment
He believed in many things that he will always be happy as he
Approach that golden road among the years of Christmas miracle
In the moment of salvation that reaches up to the Kingdom
I shall fly toward the open door of heaven with the precious
Angels and worship in the holy Christmas of peace for a little
Gift upon a shining ship as I journey toward that Blue Sea of
Praise for me to see all the citing Zion with my praise
When I prayer before the church with God
My life was important for me to pops in the precious
Wind of time as God opened his golden gate for me
To enter his city of hope with the understanding for
Me to meet a friend by hi power in faith I shall be
Improve in my way to his holy spirit of wisdom
Gene and Peter work together in the Practice of Glory
To cut down hundreds Christmas tree for the poor
Children in the need of power in a tiny miracle to come
To them as a gift in his victory of their faith that are a
Shadow in the temple of joy for them to go to a Christmas Tree farm
A risk of prayer to prepare for a star to shine all around a
Christmas tree in the wilderness of the flight of glory that
Came out of a poor soul in the Holy Power of Salvation
Peter wife Beach was place on the Holy Land of love for
The little children in Bethlehem to see the baby in holiness
They book of a play for the shepherd in the field of Bethlehem
Their journey over the Holy City of glory to see the shining
Light on the Christmas tree with the grace of faith their have
In their heart with peace that came down from heart in victory
        Hope are a large spirit in your life as you speak to the
Shepherds whom was look for away to show the law to other
In the Holy City of wisdom who need a moment of peace
For them to come out of the field into the healing power in
Prayer to dwell in the word of righteousness on the behalf

Of the living God who commend his grace to fill your heart
With a happy moment of joy to come into your life with
Salvation and live with life with him in the holy spirit of
Forgiveness
Sometimes I wept for my love one that are in heaven with
The Lord
One day I shall see you again in the loving arms of my Lord
He will give me peace in his lovingkindness someday
Beach was not a shame to show her love for everyone
In the spirit of the Lord
A strange came along with Peter to preacher his holy service
To the congregation with salvation of the kingdom in the holy
City of Bethlehem
Mark King raise up from his seat to worship in the temple
Of Victory
Jay preacher a little word on Patient that reach out to
The congregation that was heavy heart are you respond
For everything that are around you every day by the
Power in the Lord prayer of time when you step out
On the holy word that came down from the Lord
In the open air of wisdom
Gene was depressed by the state that his love one
Was going though in their life
Beach came along to talk with him on the way to the
Store in the Little Mall an hour has past and they
Have some fun together and they went back to the
Temple to speak to Jay he was talking to Jean and Lee
Need when Lance came upon them because he was a
Close friend to them and they would visit one other
When they were childhood Buddy in the past about
Five years go Lance move away for a job to Wisdom
City but he came back for a visit doing Christmas
Holiday and they was very glad to see one another
Lance wife was not with him Jay went shopping
With her mother Annie they went to Peace Mall
In the Prayer Town with her little sister Sarah Marri

So their had a good time shopping walking and
Looking at this and that in stores as they enjoy one
Another for Christmas because Christmas was a
Happy time for them because they have been
      Together for almost five years
Joy living in Victory with her family and she
One child and her name were Bless
Bless was with her husband family for the
Holiday and his family living in Bethlehem
A city of Salvation a joyful time came to you
In a moment of love in your heart
A faith in praise moment with the angels in
Heaven when you are happy in the time of
Holiness that came in midst of the temple
With all the shepherds in the wilderness
Of peace to the living God
Joy went dance around the big Christmas tree
So she could for a prayer offering in the moment
Of a summer star to shine down on you in the Holy
      Salvation of time in glory
One day you might want to enroll in the Lord
Plan that he has for you in the coverage that allow
Them to come in and out of this wicked world of sin
You make prepare for the Lord benefit that he has
For you someday in the basic of time are you cover
And included in your coming time of salvation in the
Praise dance that came into your soul of victory
The solution is your gift to the congregation of grace
In time to come to you in the holy word of the living
God as he stands by your side as you walk with him in
      Your spirit of prayer for heaven
The living God shall see in side of your heart for a
Moment of time in his precious city with peace
That he send to you for you to be happy someday
In your life that include a little moment of victory to
Help all of his spirit of grace

Sallie Big and her sister was out shopping when they
Ran into Beach Jacks, they very close in school
                When they were young
Sallie and Lucy living in the Holy City of Salvation
Sallie parents have died in a car accident about four
                        Years ago
They move back to their home town in the Holy City
                        Of Peace
Jim and his wife Bell live in a little city of Holiness, they
Takes trip around the country to see world and they went
To the Holy City of Glory and Egypt and Prayer
The weather was very nice for them as their travel to
All the city in the precious spirit of prayer on the way home
It starts to rain they had a very good trip
Jim was very glad that they took this trip to see the Holy
                        City in their life
They had plan to reach out to the needy in the spirit that
Include you by the power in the living God
A welcome plan was in the cover with your faith that someone
Made depended on your praise in the precious holiness when
You pay your vow to the Lord
Deliver your golden time with the holy angels in heaven one day
Because God had a plan for you to be a praise dance before the
Heavenly shepherd by the power in the wilderness as you select
Your faith in the church of Bethlehem with the new baby on
                            Christmas morning in the Holy City
My soul came in a way of the great moon that shine down in
The wilderness when I understand all the thing in my life with
Wisdom so I can be very happy with my family in peace say Gene
To his friend Peter I fear the power in my faith to become hole
In the present I heard a hymn come out of my heart into
The temple of my life as I march toward the Holy Land of
Salvation with the living God in the spirit of the church on
Christmas mornings I saw something shining down from the
Kingdom move me around in the Holy City of Zion
The Lord include the lost soul out in the world among

His congregation on a high mountain of prayed for to be
Heard in the field of rejoicing for your love in his salvation
Of holiness
My grace grown put of my life when it melted into a dark
Place that are passed upon a stone of glory for me open to
The Lord in Holy City for me to come hole again in his spirit
Some time I meditation on the gift of God prayer in a little
Word from heaven to give my life to him on Christmas
I shall walk a round the righteousness hill of salvation
My life is a beautiful gift to the living God when we pray
For a moment of praise to come out of my heart with grace
To the church in holiness on this holiday of Victory God shall
Guide me into his Holy City of Hope one day in the future
According to Gene heart his love went out into the world
With him when he prayer for a little moment of time
God continually to walk with me every day as I show to
His shepherds in the temple of Victory
God shall increase my glory into a vessel of redeem by
His wealth in his holy hand with prayer to feed the needy
In his power of the living God
One day God shall dwell in my life with all his shepherds
That are standing under the Christmas tree with the gift
Of Victory
A wise spirit entered the world to cheer up someone
Who are very sad according to the judgment in peace
Gene came and pour out his heart to the Lord in a vow
Of blessing when my life was against the wind in the
Dust of your temple said to his friend Peter it will be at
Fun after their depart in the spirit Gene went toward
The Holy City of Peace to Prayer for a moment of hope
In his mind as he looked back on his pass and some thing
Came back to him what happen to him on Christmas
Morning when he started to think back on his life
One Christmas he receiver a gift of love from God in
The faith with wisdom
I shall continue to praise God in the spirit of judgment

With peace for a gift to the shepherds in the Holy City
                    Of salvation
The Lord displace a prayer into the wilderness of holiness
In his love for victory he became hole again by his faith
In the church for a gift on Christmas so he received the power
In glory when he marched with the holy angels in Egypt
                    Gene mother call him to
The holy storm teacher Gene the spirit in a strange land of
Hope to cover his faith with a knowledge in victory my
Heart are fill with honey to reward the bitterness in his
Life with the love of God for me that he had by the grace
In the open wind of time that God show the world that
Rejoice in your Christmas moment of someone life
A red power came down upon a line in happiness as
I hole Gene faith close to my soul in a tiny rainbow of
Heaven for me to be at peace in my life one day soon
But some time I feel let down by everyone in my life
Say Gene I know that some day I shall be happy again
In the spirit by the power of God to everyone have a
Merry Christmas and a Happy New Year from me
                    And my family

My life are a chains of peace

Printed in the United States
By Bookmasters